Children and the Blitz

Jane Shuter

Heinemann
LIBRARY

www.heinemann.co.uk/
Visit our website to find out m   mann Library** books.

To order:
 Phone 44 (0) 1865 888066
 Send a fax to 44 (0) 1865 3140
☐ Visit the Heinemann Booksho[   ]rary to browse our
catalogue and order online.

Shuter, Jane

How do we know
about children
and the Blitz? /
                    J940.
                        531
1410564

First published in Great Britain by Heinemann
Library, Halley Court, Jordan Hill, Oxford
OX2 8EJ, part of Harcourt Education.
Heinemann is a registered trademark of Harcourt
Education Ltd.

Editorial: Lucy Thunder and Helen Cox
Design: David Poole and Geoff Ward
Illustrations: Sam Thompson at Eikon Illustration
Picture Research: Hannah Taylor
Production: Séverine Ribierre

Originated by Repro Multi Warna
Printed and bound in Hong Kong, China by
South China Printing

ISBN 0 431 12346 2
07 06 05 04 03
10 9 8 7 6 5 4 3 2 1

**British Library Cataloguing in Publicatior
Data**
Shuter, Jane
How do we know about Children and the Blitz?
941'.084
A full catalogue record for this book is available
from the British Library.

Acknowledgements
The publishers would like to thank the following
for permission to reproduce photographs:
AKG London pp**19**, **21**; Corbis/Jennie
Woodcock/Reflections Photolibrary p**18**; Hulton
Archive p**5**; Imperial War Museum (Pauline
Alwright/Mary Dunbar) p**23**; Imperial War
Museum Blitz Exhibition p**26**; John Frost
Newspapers pp**4**, **20**; Popperfoto p**25**; Robert Opi
Collection pp**22**, **27**; Tudor Photography p**24**.

Cover photograph of school children wearing gas
masks, reproduced with permission of Popperfoto

The publishers would like to thank Rebecca Vicker
for her assistance in the preparation of this book.

Every effort has been made to contact copyright
holders of any material reproduced in this book.
Any omissions will be rectified in subsequent
printings if notice is given to the publishers.

Contents

Any words shown in the text in bold, **like this**, are explained in the Glossary.

Will there be war?

Daily Express

WORLD'S LARGEST DAILY SALE

No. 11,798   Saturday, March 12, 1938   One Penny

Schuschnigg Resigns: 'I Yield To Force'

GERMANS MARCH INTO AUSTRIA

Britain And France Protest "In Strongest Possible Terms"

Mechanised Regiments Race To Vienna This Morning

FALLEN IDOL

From SYDNEY MORRELL
(Daily Express Staff Reporter)

VIENNA, Saturday Morning.

HITLER forced Dr. von Schuschnigg to resign the Chancellorship of Austria last night. The Austrian Nazis sent an SOS to Berlin for armed assistance "to avoid bloodshed." At 11.15 p.m., for the first time since the great war, man troops marched across the Austrian

Österreich

BAER WINS ON POINTS

NEW YORK, Friday.

MAX BAER won on points in his fifteen-round contest with Tommy Farr, British heavy-weight champion, in Madison-square Garden, New York, tonight.

About 18,000 people packed the hall.

Just before the fight the odds lengthened to 2 to 1 on Farr, owing to the shortage of money for Baer. At the weigh-in the afternoon Farr had turned the scales at 14st. 12½lbs. and Baer at 15st. 2lbs.

ROUND ONE.—The crowd was in an intense state of excitement as Baer came out of his corner and pounded three right uppercuts to the body. They fought at close quarters, and Farr got in three left jabs to the head.

The spectators roared as they saw that Baer had no defence against

was forced to cover up under a barrage of punches to the head, but caught Farr with a right to the head.

This was Farr's round.

ROUND ELEVEN.—Baer drove Farr across the ring.

Baer cuffed Farr half across the ring with a left to the head after landing right punches with both hands to the body. Tommy came back and drove Baer into a corner. This was Baer's round.

ROUND TWELVE.—Baer caught Farr with one under the ear as Farr jabbed his face in return. Farr scored hard blows to the chin with each hand.

This was Farr's round.

ROUND THIRTEEN. Farr landed

LATEST NEWS
Telephone: Central 8000

HITLER OVER AUSTRIA
Daily Express Staff Reporter

Berlin, Saturday.—Announcement of a united Austro-German Reich, with Hitler as leader, will be made today by Propaganda Minister Dr. Goebbels.

A proclamation by Chancellor Hitler will speak today of the two peoples and the world's foundation of new great Nazi Reich.

Poison Tablets Left On Bus Seat

In 1938, Adolf Hitler, the German leader, ordered his armies to **invade** other European countries. The British **government** feared that only a war might stop them.

4

The government was worried that as soon as war broke out, the Germans would bomb Britain. Before the war started they prepared for bombing.

Preparing for war

The **government** gave everyone **gas masks**, in case the German bombs carried poisonous gas. People built **bomb shelters** in their gardens.

War broke out on 3 September 1939. **ARP wardens** checked that people hid lights at night with **blackout curtains**. They made sure each house had one room safe from bombs.

Evacuation

Cities were the most likely places to be bombed. In September 1939, the British **government** began to **evacuate** children to safety. Whole schools were evacuated.

The **evacuees** went to live with **host families** in the countryside. Children from big families were often split up. Sometimes they felt sad and lonely.

Staying home

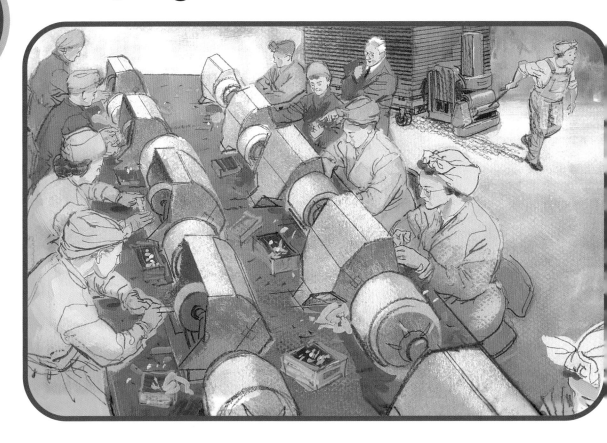

Some children stayed in London. Their families refused to **evacuate** them. These children spent a lot of time alone, as their families were away fighting or out working.

By December 1939, Britain had not yet been bombed. Many **evacuees** spent Christmas at home. People thought the Germans would not bomb them.

Blitz!

On 7 September 1940, the Germans started bombing British cities. They bombed mostly at night. London's first **air raid** was by 400 German bomber planes.

This was called the Blitz. 'Blitz' is short for the German word *Blitzkrieg*, which means 'lightning war'. About 138,000 people were killed or wounded in German air raids during the Blitz.

Living through it

Children were often woken at night to go to **bomb shelters**. Thousands of people slept in the London **Underground** during **air raids**.

The Blitz caused terrible damage.
Homes were flattened and people had
to move in with family or friends.
Many more children were **evacuated**.

After the Blitz

The London Blitz ended in May 1941. Most **evacuees** went home to the cities. The war ended in May 1945, when Germany **surrendered**.

The Blitz had destroyed many homes. After the war, the **government** built temporary homes called **prefabs**. Homeless people lived in them until new homes were ready.

Memories of war

One important way of finding out about the Blitz is to talk to people who were there. Now, children can talk to people who were children then.

Some of the people who flew the German bomber planes are still alive. They remember the Blitz as well, and can talk about their memories.

Newspapers and photos

Newspapers printed stories and photos of the bombings. The **government** stopped them from printing the worst pictures. It thought people might not support the war if they saw them.

Photos taken at the time show what the Blitz was like. This is one of the few colour photos taken, because colour film was new and very expensive.

Posters and paintings

The **government** stuck up posters to encourage people to **evacuate** their children during the Blitz. This poster tells parents to keep their children in the countryside.

Many artists painted pictures of life during the war. Some painted the fighting abroad. This painting shows nurses travelling away from the war.

War objects

Many **artefacts** have survived from the time of the Blitz. This picture shows a **gas mask**, a pair of **binoculars** and a **tin hat**.

Radios were an important way of telling people war news. We can still listen to speeches made by the prime minister, Winston Churchill, during the Blitz.

Museums

Many **museums** have displays that show us what life was like during the Blitz. London's Imperial War Museum has something called the 'Blitz Experience', shown here.

Museums also show us what people ate during the Blitz. From January 1940 food was **rationed** in Britain. People could only buy set amounts each week.

Timeline

1938 The British **government** gives out over 38 million **gas masks**.

1 September 1939 The German army **invades** Poland. The British government begins to **evacuate** children from the cities.

3 September 1939 Britain, France, Australia and New Zealand go to war with Germany. This is called World War II. By this time about 1.5 million children have been evacuated.

December 1939 Many children go home for Christmas and do not go back to the countryside.

8 January 1940 Butter, sugar, bacon and ham are **rationed**.

7 September 1940 Germany begins bombing Britain. London is 'Blitzed' by daily bombing.

14 November 1940 Germans bomb Coventry. Liverpool, Bristol and Southampton are bombed in the next few weeks.

May 1941 Fewer **air raids**. The Blitz ends. There are more bombing raids later, but they are not part of the Blitz.

7 May 1945 Germany **surrenders** and the war in Europe ends.

Biographies

Winston Churchill

Winston Churchill was born in Blenheim Palace, near Oxford, in 1874. He was made prime minister in May 1940 and led the government all through the war. Winston's speeches on the radio kept people full of hope through the Blitz. He died in 1965.

Adolf Hitler

Adolf Hitler was born in Austria in 1889. In 1933, Adolf and his **Nazi Party** took power in Germany. Adolf and the Nazis wanted to make Germany a big, powerful country. So, they invaded other countries in Europe. This led to World War II (1939–45). Adolf shot himself on 30 April 1945, when Germany lost the war.

An evacuee – Ben Wicks

Ben Wicks was born in 1927. He lived in London, and was evacuated at the age of twelve to Eastbourne, on the south coast. His whole school went with him. Ben went back to London just before his fifteenth birthday and joined the army when he was seventeen years old. He wrote a book about **evacuees** called *No Time to Wave Goodbye*.

Glossary

air raid attack by many bomber planes

ARP warden short for Air Raid Precaution warden. Wardens were taught what things to do to in an air raid and made sure everyone did them.

artefact object that is made by humans

binoculars an object that makes things look bigger when you look through it. It has two barrels to look through, one for each eye.

blackout curtains curtains that fitted tightly over windows and doors so that no light showed outside

bomb shelter place where people hid away from bombing during air raids

evacuate to send a person away from their home for their own safety

evacuee someone who is evacuated

gas mask mask worn over the head that makes poisonous air safe to breathe

government people who run a country

host families families who offered, or were made, to take evacuees into their homes

invade to send an army into another country to take it over and rule it. This is called an invasion.

museum building that has things in it that tell us about the past

Nazi Party political party that took power in Germany in 1933. It was led by Adolf Hitler.

prefabs houses that were made all the same size and shape and could be put up in half a day. Prefab is short for 'prefabricated house'.

rationed only allowed in very limited amounts

surrender to give up fighting in a war

tin hat helmet made from steel that was worn by emergency service workers and volunteers, such as ARP wardens

Underground the London Underground train service, which runs in tunnels under the city

Further reading

The Blitz, Andrew Langley, Hamlyn, 1995

The Blitz, John Simkin, Spartacus, 1987

Evacuees, Carolyn Sloan, Ginn, 1995

Index

Titles in the *How Do we Know About ...?* series include:

Hardback   0 431 12344 6

Hardback   0 431 12346 2

Hardback   0 431 12345 4

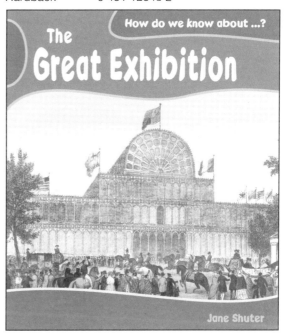

Hardback   0 431 12347 0

Find out about the other titles in this series on our website www.heinemann.co.uk/library